DISTURBING THE CALM

A Memoir of Time and Place

BY
Judith Barker Kvinsland

KITSAP PUBLISHING

Disturbing the Calm: A Memoir of Time and Place
First edition, published 2020

By Judith Barker Kvinsland

Copyright © 2020, Judith Barker Kvinsland

Cover photo by Ryan Wu on Unsplash

Paperback ISBN-13: 978-1-942661-51-1

All rights reserved. No part of this book may be reproduced or transmitted in any form or by any means, electronic or mechanical, including photocopying, recording or by any information storage and retrieval system, without written permission from the author, except for the inclusion of brief quotations in a review.

Published by Kitsap Publishing
Poulsbo, WA 98370
www.KitsapPublishing.com

Contents

Part One. Home: Before We Knew it was the Salish Sea 1
Chapter 1: My Birth in Two Takes 3
Chapter 2: The Art of Scrabbling 7
Chapter 3: Grave Tenders 12
Chapter 4: Visionaries 20
Chapter 5: Game On 25

Part Two. Leaving: Uncharted Territory 33
Chapter 6: No Way of Knowing 35
Chapter 7: Best-laid Plans 42
Chapter 8: A Day, Unlike Any Other 46
Chapter 9: The Question 51
Chapter 10: Uncharted Territory 54

Part Three. Changes: Disturbing the Calm 61
Chapter 11: Disturbing the Calm 63
Chapter 12: A Reason for Flight 68
Chapter 13: The Promise 71
Chapter 14: Doc Speak 75
Chapter 15: Look Back 80

Acknowledgments 87
Additional Acknowledgments 89
Biography 91

Dedication

To my parents and grandparents; for their unconditional love and continuous support.

"Instructions for living a life:
Pay attention.
Be astonished.
Tell about it."

- From the poem, *"Sometimes,"* by Mary Oliver

Part One

Home: Before We Knew it was the Salish Sea

1

My Birth in Two Takes

As American and British troops pushed their way through France—one year to the day before the end of World War II—my mother went into labor. My father was nowhere near.

During my childhood, I often pestered my parents to relive that day. I relished hearing their versions of my birthdate—problematic for my mother—because she was not only alone, but there was a shortage of doctors in Bremerton, available to deliver me during wartime at Franklin Delano Roosevelt Hospital. Imagine her anguish when the doctor-on-call that Labor Day weekend—an eye, ear, nose, and throat specialist—arrived, assessed the scene, and mumbled, "Well, you sure look ready. I'm not quite sure I know what to do." My birth was further complicated by the American Red Cross who sent the wrong information in a telegram—following my delivery—to my father who was training Army troops at Fort Wheeler, Georgia.

Classic Mom-Speak:

"Tell me about the day I was born," I begged my mother when she worked at her command post before our kitchen sink, busily involved in a household task. I leaned my cat-scratched forearms upon the linoleum countertop and looked up expectantly, always wondering if her story might vary.

In addition to what must have been a painful experience for her—due to the lack of expertise that accompanied my birth—my mother's recollections also lacked a filter, a gentler way of sharing her recollections with her listener. What I later referred to as, "Classic-Mom-Speak," was her direct style of communication, inherited from her straightforward, tell-it-like-it-is, immigrant Norwegian parents. Just the facts.

"You were huge. You looked like a prizefighter, a real heavyweight," she mused. It was not until years later when my parents bought the Encyclopedia Americana from a door-to-door salesman that I discovered the word *heavyweight*. I stared at the picture of a boxer and learned what a prizefighter looked like.

I was devastated by her story.

Did this mean that I was born jabbing and punching?

Did I have huge muscles in my arms?

What about my stomach? Was it soft and smooth, or was it rippled, like the boxer in the picture? After all, I did weigh nine pounds.

My mother was always vague when I pressed her for more details. I think she eventually realized that her original story was less than satisfying for me. One day, she modified it, "Oh, you just had a lot of hair, long and thick. You had so much hair that I had to give you a haircut as soon as I took you home." Obviously, when the popular vocalist, Bing Crosby, crooned, "You must have been a beautiful baby," he was not thinking of me.

Decades later, my parents came to visit me in the hospital, shortly after I gave birth to my daughter, amidst skilled support services and medical expertise. My mother was elated. She kissed me before she left and whispered in my ear, "I'm so glad you had a girl first. Just like I did. She's so beautiful. Just like you were."

A Different Take:

My father's memories of that weekend were different. I usually snagged his attention when he was hunkered down, beneath the hood of our family Chevy. Checking the radiator. Checking the oil. Searching for loose connections. Tightening up bolts when he discovered a culprit.

He always cooperated when I asked, "Do you still remember the day I was born?"

He was a thoughtful man, a Virginian, who always considered the impact of his words before he spoke. He stopped what he was doing and gave me his full attention.

"Well, the Red Cross contacted me there in Georgia at Fort Wheeler. We were training troops, getting ready to end that War. You know, I was on my way over there too, but then you were born. At that time, they only sent soldiers overseas who didn't have children.

A Red Cross volunteer found me and handed me a telegram, 'You have a son,'" he recalled.

"I was so happy that day. You know, a son carries the family name forward into the next generation. I liked thinking about that. A few days later they handed me another telegram, this time from your mother: 'I named her Judith Louise.'"

Dad always chuckled at that point in his story. He emerged from under the hood and carefully wiped his hands on the tattered, terry cloth towel he always carried in his back pocket, just in case something needed cleaning.

"I sure was confused, but it's been just fine with me. You'll always be my firstborn, that boy who turned out to be a girl. I've never regretted it one bit!"

In the 1950's and 1960's, in the rural community where I grew up on Puget Sound, money for college was scarce. Some families prioritized college tuition for their sons. After all, tradition suggested they were going to be heads of households. Girls often went to secretarial schools to perfect their typing, while boys went to college to prepare for life.

Years later, I overheard one of my aunts admonish my father, "Why are you sending Judy to college? You should save your money and send the boys."

My father was outraged. "All of my children are going to college," he countered, "my daughters, as well as my sons."

Maybe he remembered that telegram, "You have a son." It was the only occasion, that I can recall, that my father treated me like one of the boys. He made it clear, "I was just fine with him."

2

The Art of Scrabbling

In 1950, my parents bought our family home, a fifty-year-old, shingled craftsman perched on a hillside overlooking the Washington State Ferry terminal in Harper. In that single move, I acquired my own bedroom, an intriguing, elderly neighbor who asked us to call her, "Aunt Margaret," and a standing invitation for me to play Scrabble in her dining room, any time I wanted. I was thrilled, even though I could barely read.

My six-year-old self did not readily realize that Aunt Margaret had owned and lived in the house that my parents bought and settled into with me and my younger brother. Our home had been Aunt Margaret's home. Our sweeping view of Puget Sound, Blake Island, and West Seattle had been her view. Our wall of bookshelves that we filled with a growing collection of Little Golden Books and childhood classics—like <u>Little Women</u> and <u>Heidi</u>, among others—had been her bookshelves.

Before we moved in, Aunt Margaret downsized into a smaller, more compact house she also owned, on the north edge of our property line. Widowed as a young woman, she had no children, never remarried, welcomed us as extended family, and established a relationship that lasted for the next twenty years while we were neighbors in that peaceful community on the Olympic Peninsula.

Aunt Margaret was tall, a head taller than my mom and all of my aunts. She was bulky and shapeless. Every day, she formally dressed in a stiff, dark, gabardine dress, even though she wasn't going anywhere, other than our laid-back neighborhood. She always wore thick, cotton hosiery and chunky-heeled white or black pumps, depending upon the season. Comfortable with her size and bearing, Aunt Margaret accented her image with bold, fanciful—and from my perspective—glamorous jewelry; strands of coral beads, heavy gold and silver bracelets, gaudy, pinky rings, and sparkling, rhinestone, clip-back earrings.

Aunt Margaret owned a pure white, short-haired cat named "Kitty Kitsap," named in honor of the county where we lived. Unlike my series of cats and kittens—who were "Garage Cats" and huddled together outside at night—Kitty Kitsap slept indoors before the fireplace, on a fluffy pillow. When awake, the pampered cat presided over her territory perched on the couch, the window sill, or on Aunt Margaret's ample lap, a behavior that I soon discovered after I decided to take Aunt Margaret up on her offer to play Scrabble.

When I wasn't in school, or rushing through my list of chores—dusting furniture, drying dishes, and sweeping our kitchen floor—which I considered to be drudgery, I raced down the hill to Aunt Margaret's. Over time, I developed the habit of neglecting my tasks to spend as much time playing Scrabble as I could. Avoiding my mother's ever-watchful eyes, I skipped out of dusting our bookshelves, left the breakfast dishes in a rack to air dry, and often left my bed unmade. My mother sighed in frustration, but let me go.

I slipped inside Aunt Margaret's house through the back door—we had become that familiar—and called out, "I'm here." I headed for the dining room and slid onto a hard wooden chair, ready to pick up the game, right where we had stopped during our previous session. Aunt Margaret never put away her wooden Scrabble board. It was a permanent fixture on her dining room table, its wooden surface, smoothed and worn, after years of use.

With Kitty Kitsap purring on her lap, Aunt Margaret always began, "I think it is your turn." Hunched over the board, I studied the tray of tiles before me and struggled to remember what word I had on my mind before we had stopped, usually because my mother sent my brother down to inform me, "Dinner's ready. You need to come home. Now."

Aunt Margaret was patient. Aunt Margaret was encouraging, but she was also tough and expected me to stretch up to play at her level, showing little mercy or inclination to dumb down the game. Fortunately, I learned to read quickly and easily. Most of the time, I could hold my own which provided me endless opportunities to practice what I knew. I also learned to take chances with my rudimentary knowledge, risked putting out odd concoctions of letters, hoping she would verify their validity.

She always spun the board her way and scrutinized my combination of letters. I waited expectantly. If I was right, she smiled and said, "Good for you," and added points to my tally. I grinned and leaned over to pat Kitty Kitsap, who did not share the joy of my accomplishment. She usually hissed at me, then resumed her nap.

If my attempt appeared flimsy, Aunt Margaret slid her giant dictionary—that rested between us—across the table and challenged me to verify my offering. I held my breath and pored through its pages searching for my creation. When I couldn't find it, I sadly lifted the tiles off of the board and returned them to my tray. Not wanting to lose my turn, I plopped a two-or-three-lettered, low-point, safe word on the board and moved on. It was Aunt Margaret's turn.

Those moments challenged me, but they developed my competitive spirit, and I always believed I could do better on my next try. Over time, my odd concoctions turned out to be valid, and they became part of my vocabulary. The game of Scrabble—that Aunt Margaret and I played together for most of my childhood and early adolescence—not only developed my vocabulary, but confidence in my ability to learn, and tackle new challenges.

I left Harper in 1962 to attend college at Pacific Lutheran University. As a first-generation college student, I pored over the official "College Needs" list sent by the Office of Admissions and followed it carefully. After all, what did I know about the needs of a college student? Everything I knew, I had gleaned from the College Edition of "Mademoiselle Magazine," published every August. I carefully packed box after box of recommended essentials. Just before I left, I slipped in Aunt Margaret's high school graduation gift: the latest edition of <u>Merriam-Webster's Collegiate Dictionary and Complete Thesaurus</u>.

Late at night during my freshman year, I longed for my home and family. I felt forlorn, overwhelmed, and was often tearful in my cramped dorm room, hunched over an assignment due the next day, but I was able to persevere. Fortified with the love, encouragement, and endless sacrifices of my parents, the countless hours I spent with Aunt Margaret instilled in me a store of confidence and strength. It kept me going. It caused me to stretch up to play at a new level, on my way to the woman I could become.

3

Grave Tenders

I knew my way around Sedgwick Cemetery. I come from a family of grave tenders. We were not professionals, but earnest plot-raking, flower-arranging, fern-pulling people. We practiced our craft in a family plot in the middle of a rural cemetery, established in 1910 by descendants of Union Army veterans who drifted westward to Puget Sound country. The east coast transplants envisioned the peaceful, Kitsap County meadow—surrounded by towering evergreen firs and cedars—as potential burial sites for their families. These newcomers could never have predicted that a succession of immigrants, mostly stalwart Norwegians like my grandparents, would eventually gravitate toward Sedgwick Cemetery and hallow its ground.

In the early 1950's, when I was nine-years-old, I overheard my grandparents and their Norwegian neighbors complain, "Someone stole all of our flower arrangements—every single one of them—right off of the graves at Sedgwick!"

Perched atop a staircase, I peered down and eavesdropped upon their late summer gathering in my grandparents' parlor. My family lived nearby. I visited my grandparents often, happily roamed their farm, and helped Grandma serve coffee and cookies to guests, usually immigrants, like themselves.

"Imagine that," they muttered.

"Nay, why would people steal 'tings' like that?" They jabbered away in their unique language, a casual mishmash of both English and Norwegian.

"Besides that, dogs are 'shetten' right there on the graves, leaving their mess on our plots!" Shaking their heads, they collectively clucked their tongues in disgust over such unthinkable actions.

The next spring, I learned just how much the local Norwegians had been offended by the unknown intruders. My grandpa picked me up—just before Memorial Day—in his ancient Oldsmobile, and we chugged off to conduct the annual cleanup of our family plot. Grandpa wore his customary work clothes: khaki pants, starched and ironed by my grandma; a wool, plaid work shirt, that was often a Christmas gift from a grandchild; a brimmed, fisherman's cap to protect his shiny, bald head from the sun; and laceless boots. Entering my grandparents' tidy home required the removal of one's shoes. The absence of laces hastened that task for Grandpa as he tromped in and out of their farmhouse for coffee breaks and mid-day dinner. Grandpa had ruddy cheeks that often held a chaw of Copenhagen snuff—stashed there, comfortably—while he went about his busy day.

As we approached the entrance to Sedgwick Cemetery, a large iron gate greeted us. Grandpa quickly braked. Without a seatbelt—not yet mandated by law—I flew forward and bumped my head against the windshield. After the sudden jolt, I rubbed my sore forehead, as Grandpa gently patted my back, a gesture that almost always lessened my random, childhood hurts.

The boldest of the community's Norwegians had installed the gate over the winter to protect their beloved plots at Sedgwick Cemetery. I badgered Grandpa, "How do your friends think they can keep burglars out of here? Sure, it's a new gate, but just look at this old fence. See the huge holes in it. Even bears, if they wanted to, could wander in through openings this big. Dogs can still get in, too. Dogs aren't stupid!"

Grandpa silently studied the gate. As we sat there, I recalled a child's adaptation of the spooky story, "The Legend of Sleepy Hollow." I scoffed, "It feels creepy here. Haven't your friends ever heard of the Headless Horseman, that guy from Sleepy Hollow, who rides out of his grave looking for his missing head? A horse could make it here from Sleepy Hollow. Horses can jump over fences and gates!"

I finally quieted down, but at the same time realized that I really didn't like Sedgwick Cemetery very much. It made me sad. I never saw anyone smile here. If we ever encountered others during our annual chores, I noticed them wiping their reddened eyes and sniveling into a white handkerchief that someone in their family had washed and ironed for them.

On previous visits, Grandpa encouraged me to be especially nice when we passed by grieving folks. I tried. I softly crept up next to them and attempted to attract their attention.

"Hello. Can I get some water for your vase? I know a shortcut to the faucet, way over there," I pointed to the lone water source in the cemetery. "I can fill up that vase. By the way, I like your flowers. Are they bluebells?" I chattered.

On those occasions, I quickly exhausted my store of kindness, as well as my rudimentary knowledge of gardening. I encountered only staunch Norwegians, stalwart folks who hastily wiped their eyes, stuffed their soiled handkerchiefs into a pocket, and regained their stoic personas, without my help.

"Now, go out there and open up that gate for me, would ya?" Grandpa sighed and ignored my graveyard rant. I could barely hear his voice above the clamor of the Oldsmobile's engine. Feeling indignant—with another chore added to my annual tasks—I shoved the heavy car door open. I hopped barefoot, down into the dust, careful to avoid any shards of rocks that might cut my feet. Just one more week of school, and I would be free. I was in training—toughening up the soles of my feet—so I could run barefoot and enjoy a summer reprieve from scuffed-up, saddle shoes and knee-high socks.

I slowly slid my fingers along the top of the iron gate and watched the winter accumulation of burnt umber, iron flakes float softly to the ground. I reached for the latch, but I found it stuck, already rusted by the steady patter of northwest rain. I tugged and tugged until one successful pull shattered the layers of rust and set the gate free. I jumped back—out of its path—as the iron mass creaked open. It groaned as it lurched by me, where I stood flattened against one of the aged fence posts that held the gate in check. Grandpa's Oldsmobile roared forward with a growl.

"Close it behind me, will ya?" Grandpa shouted as he sailed by, leaving me enveloped in a putrid trail of exhaust, spurting from the car's crusty tailpipe. I waved my arms back and forth to dispel the stench. "Ugh!" I admonished the belching cloud as I flapped my arms amidst the fumes.

Suddenly, a second cloud of choking dust—stirred up by Grandpa's tires, as he trundled along the narrow track that circled the cemetery—swirled about me. I held my breath until the dust floated away. I had already depleted my energy, flapping my arms.

I took my time. I sauntered along behind Grandpa's car and followed the rutted route to our family plot. Tufts of sweet, spring grass separated well-worn tire tracks, a welcome respite for the soles of my not-yet-toughened-up feet. I thought about the raspberry Kool-Aid in the quart jar my grandma had packed for us. I could feel it sliding down my throat, cool and sweet.

I ambled along cautiously, imagining the Headless Horseman, who might loom up from behind tall, leafy bushes that some Norwegians had planted on the graves of their loved ones. They wanted their graveside displays to be permanent and harder to steal. But unknown intruders still dug them up.

We tended graves that belonged to people who I had never met: my grandparents' firstborn, Agnes, who died of meningitis as a child; my great-aunt Signe, her husband, and their two children, all taken by tuberculosis, long before my birth. As a child, I could not yet foresee the succession of burials that would bring me back to Sedgwick Cemetery in the years ahead.

As grave tenders, we engaged in genuine, hard work. Every year, we tugged at the vast accumulation of woody-stemmed, fiddlehead ferns that overwintered in our plot. These nasty visitors flourished like the contents of a Petri dish, nourished by endless moisture during Washington winters. Before I started pulling my share of ferns, I usually wandered around and searched for new graves, hopefully, timing my arrival after Grandpa finished the disagreeable task. If I was lucky, I could arrive just in time for the Kool-Aid break. Then I could arrange the abundance of colorful flowers from Grandpa's garden and place them on the gravestones, my favorite part of grave tending. I had already transformed Hills Brothers' coffee cans into vases, covering them with aluminum foil—in my eyes, a grand accomplishment.

Grandpa always launched our annual cleanup by weeding and tending to the grave of my Aunt Agnes, my grandparents' eldest daughter. She died when she was only nine. I found him kneeling there when I strolled up next to him, that May afternoon.

"Do you still miss her, Grandpa?" I asked as he gently scrubbed away another year's growth of moss from her aged, cement tombstone. As a child, how could I have known the feelings and memories I might thoughtlessly have reopened for him? He hesitated before responding, "Yah, I sure do," he whispered. After a long pause, Grandpa added, "Now run along and get me that hammer in my toolbox," as he knelt a bit longer by Agnes' grave.

As I searched for his hammer, I spied a fresh grave across the cemetery, so recent that it still had a pile of damp dirt mounded over it. I dropped the hammer near Grandpa and tiptoed through the open space until I reached the new grave. A large wreath of once-brilliant, crimson roses had already disintegrated into dust, but a whiff of their sweet, gentle fragrance remained. I poked at the petals with a stick and watched the dusky powder float about me in the slight breeze. Red velvet ribbons appeared to be the only part of the wreath left unscathed by time and nature. I thought to myself, "Maybe, I could just take these ribbons home with me?" Taking them seemed easy enough. I could tie them in my doll's hair, or even better, fashion a collar for my cat.

I glanced around to see if Grandpa could see me. Now that he had finished tending to Agnes' grave, he was busily repairing the low fence that defined our family plot, his hammer rhythmically shattering the afternoon silence. "Tap, tap, tap," he worked his way around the rectangle of our loved ones, mending the small sagging breaks in the perimeter of the plot. Even though he couldn't see me, I reconsidered my plan. I didn't want to be one of those grave robbers, scolded later, by local Norwegians.

I bent down to read the small, stark placard—a temporary identification of the dead—that had been pounded into the soft ground: Philip Long, 1944-1953. Just my age. I jumped back and gasped. I burst into tears.

I realized that the age-old, childhood prayer that I prayed every night could actually come true: "Now I lay me down to sleep, and pray Thee Lord, my soul to keep. If I should die, before I wake, I pray Thee Lord, my soul to take." Every night before bedtime, I rushed through the first part of that prayer, in a hurry to reach the second stanza, that I liked better: "If I should live for other days, I pray Thee Lord, to guide my ways."

Nine-year-olds, like me, could actually die in their sleep before waking! My aunt Agnes had died when she was only nine, and so had this child, Philip. The thought overwhelmed me. I cried even harder. In fact, I sobbed uncontrollably. I ran toward my grandpa, who was unfolding himself upward, from all fours to a standing position. He dropped his hammer and spun around to see what had happened to me.

I jumped over the newly repaired fence. I hugged his girth with gratitude and stammered through my tears, "Grandpa, are there any of those ferns left for me to pull?" Suddenly, all I wanted was to work hard and be there beside my grandpa. "Please, Grandpa?" I continued, "I'm so happy, so happy to be here with you."

I added my share of pulled ferns to the pile he had already begun. I placed my childish arrangements beside each of the grave markers, reserving the most colorful and largest for my Aunt Agnes. Grandpa and I stood back together and admired our work. Standing there side by side, pleased with our efforts, there was no way that we could have known that in just a short time, my grandpa's grave would be added to our family plot and require tending.

4

Visionaries

On a spring evening at the end of my sophomore year of high school, my father and I entered unknown territory. Like explorers—not quite certain of the landscape before us—we paused outside of my school cafeteria, the site of the annual National Honor Society banquet and induction ceremony. Even though we were late, we hesitated, unsure of what to do. We were unfamiliar with banquets. We were unfamiliar with honor societies.

We stood there out of breath—seemingly, the last to arrive—after running a half-mile up Mitchell Hill since the school parking lot was full. Even though my father had left his marine construction job on the Duwamish River early, he still had to navigate Seattle streets during rush hour, hop on a Washington state ferry, pick me up at our home, and maneuver miles of country roads to get us here. I glanced down at the invitation clutched in my hand, making sure we were in the right place.

I surveyed my new shoes, to see if I had damaged their tiny heels during our sprint. I smoothed the skirt of the flowered cotton, A-line dress I had sewn the weekend before. I had carefully following the directions of a Vogue pattern that mimicked the dresses Jackie Kennedy had worn during her husband's campaign for the Presidency.

My father and I peeked inside the cafeteria nearly filled to capacity with chattering students—most, I had known since kindergarten—seated alongside their proud parents. I perked up when several of my friends waved at me. My father nodded at a few of our neighbors, fellow commuters, like himself.

Dad's breathing quickly stabilized. He was in good shape—his body, trim and lean—honed by long shifts jumping from docks to decks, scrambling up iron ladders to pilot a tugboat on the inland waters of Puget Sound. My mother stayed home that evening to care for my younger brothers, but Dad cut short his workday to be here with me. I gazed at him with gratitude.

"Are we ready?" Dad asked, squeezed my arm, and led me in. We threaded our way through the tightly spaced tables that filled the cafeteria. I tightly clutched his arm to avoid slipping on the slick floor, in my spindly heels. I could sense that my dad—the son of a tenant farmer in Virginia—was beginning to relax and feel comfortable. He had only been able to progress as far as the sixth grade before he—one of eleven children—was needed to contribute to the farm and household chores. As we navigated across the cafeteria, he reached out and vigorously shook hands as we passed by our neighbors or a fellow commuter from the Washington state ferry that chugged out of Harper every weekday morning at 5:50 a.m.

I nodded to my friends, smiled at their moms and dads, and searched for a place to sit. At last, I spotted the only two seats left in the room. Dad and I quickly slipped into the empty folding chairs and prepared to dine right in front of the illustrious locals at the head table. Dad and I exchanged glances and sat up a bit straighter.

I nibbled at some of the celebratory dinner, which actually turned out to be our usual lunchroom fare. For this occasion, the school cooks had dressed up each plate with a canned crabapple—its stem, intact—and several sprigs of parsley that added an air of festivity. I took a few bites of what was listed on the program as Salisbury Steak and wondered what my mother was preparing at home. If Dad also wondered, he gave me no clue. He dug into his meal with vigor.

As I slowly munched my way through a cookie, the best part of the meal, I began to study the membership of the head table. All of them were males; every student leader, every teacher, every administrator, all males. My eyes roved back and forth, flitting from one dark suit and tie to another dark suit and tie.

The glaring predominance of males in leadership had never been so clear, so graphic, so dramatically visible to me before this evening. Suddenly, I caught a glimpse of color, a shimmer of pastel, far down the head table to my right. I leaned forward, stared boldly, and tried to identify the stranger, the lone female among the all-male lineup.

I was still staring at her when our popular, new principal stood up to introduce the head table. After what seemed to be a long time, he gazed away, far down the table, and completed his task, "I would like to introduce my wife." Everyone applauded. It was his wife—dressed in pastel hues—who shimmered at the end of the table.

One by one, the male speakers came forward. My mind drifted away as they droned on. I began to think about my life. There was a rhythm, a predictability to each day, as I hauled textbooks and binders up and down the three flights of stairs of our old brick high school. Every fifty-five minutes, classroom bells assaulted our eardrums, and teachers ordered all eight hundred of us—including some who had daydreamed away the previous hour—to "Get up. Move on. Don't dawdle."

In just a short time, I had perfected the drill of high school.

I maintained a 4.0 average, plus an invitation to tonight's National Honor Society induction ceremony and banquet.

I was a bookworm, in love with learning. I adored reading <u>Great Expectations,</u> <u>Silas Marner,</u> and <u>Les Miserables</u>, although I wouldn't admit that to my peers. When I wasn't reading the classics, I shifted my interest to Holden Caulfield, who I met in <u>The Catcher in the Rye</u>.

I had earned the sole sophomore spot on the girls' traveling tennis team.

I had been elected cheerleader for the upcoming year.

I had a steady boyfriend—who was the junior class president and a three-sport letterman—as well as an invitation to the junior prom.

Even though everything in my life seemed just right, I still wanted more. I was beginning to hope for change, something different than the lives I observed around me, but was uncertain of how to disturb the calm and make things happen.

I turned my attention back to the head table when the principal rose again and encouraged the new inductees to aspire to new levels, to achieve new things. I listened carefully.

Amidst the excitement of his words, something shifted that evening, as if I had found a new direction, the inspiration to take a new pathway.

I leaned over and whispered, "Dad, I'm going to college. Someday I'm going to be sitting up there. I'm going to be sitting at the head table. You'll see." My dad sat there beaming, as if we had just taken possession of a new land, no longer explorers, but visionaries.

I filled the remainder of my high school years with activities and actions that would prepare me to go to college, to be the first person—in the history of my family—to have that opportunity, unaware that I was also setting the bar for my brothers and sister, nieces and nephews, and eventually, my own children and grandchildren.

My father died in 2008, nearly fifty years after the evening. All of his life, he delighted in those moments at the banquet. He told the story of my dream, over and over again. Every time I earned a degree, accomplished a goal, or took advantage of an opportunity, Dad smiled, "That little girl told me a long time ago that she was going to be sitting at the head table, and sure enough, she made it. She said she was going to be the leader of a school someday, and she did it."

I never admitted to Dad the limitations of my vision that evening. After all, I had never seen a woman in a leadership role. As a fifteen-year-old female in a world led by men, I assumed that if I went to college, I would find a husband there who would be successful, and through him, I might sit at the head table someday. I had only aspired to be the glimmer of pastel at the end of the table.

That evening, my Dad saw something more. He envisioned that his daughter could break traditional barriers, accomplish anything she wanted to do. He saw me as the principal, perhaps the superintendent.

"Why not?" His can-do attitude swept over me like a flood. He set the bar higher, and I reached up.

5

Game On

"Whack!" I heard Sue's tennis racket collide with the ball she had just tossed high overhead. I crouched low and waited on the left half of our makeshift tennis court—a court that we measured out and chalk-lined daily—on the school bus turnaround behind our high school gym, that spring afternoon in 1960.

"Ball in play!" our grey-haired coach yelled. Her shout alerted me that Sue had nailed the sweet spot on the brick wall, slightly above the chalk line that replicated the height of a real court's net. I rose up on my toes and twirled my wooden Wilson racket around in my sweaty palms. I swayed back and forth, ready to lunge left or right, depending upon which way the ball ricocheted. Years of constant use, by heavy school buses, left sharp rocks exposed—amidst the uneven asphalt—which added additional challenges to our improvised tennis court.

"Thwok!" I slammed the ball back to the brick wall as hard as I could, relying upon a forehand, my better shot. Game on.

Sue—who towered six inches above me and outweighed me by fifty pounds—was a formidable opponent. Her tanned forearms were well muscled, in contrast to my own skinny ones, but I lived near a neighborhood tennis court and could always find someone—usually a boy, stronger than me, and more skilled—to volley back and forth most afternoons. I learned to play defensively, move quickly, and hit the ball deep to force a stronger opponent away from the net.

"Whoosh!" Sue's return whizzed past my ears.

We narrowed our eyes and tracked each shot as it rapidly approached us. We placed the ball to the left, then aimed to the right. We hit softly and forced each other forward; then mobilized our skills to land the next shot far back—toward the rear chalk line—hoping to catch each other off guard. We focused our eyes on the dusty brick wall, as we battled weekly to earn the lone, sophomore spot on the girl's tennis team.

Our teammates shagged our stray balls as they watched the action, waiting their turns on the less-than-desirable court. A few gazed wistfully down the hill at the boys' tennis team, happily practicing on the high school's two, yellow-lined, fenced courts.

Our team persevered, a decade before federally mandated Title IX legislation provided girls equal access to participate and play on high school and college facilities. We only practiced on the real courts, if the boys played an away-match, or if it rained, and they canceled their turnout. Fortunately, we gained access to the courts when our school hosted visiting teams, but our matches were secondary to the boys' schedule. Boys played first. We were left behind in the gathering dusk to play our opponents. I guess we could have called ourselves, "The Lady Wolves," but we hadn't yet envisioned that kind of fame or notoriety. Only the boys' team received any press in the local newspaper. Our team was not only court-less but nameless.

I beat Sue that afternoon—as I somehow did each week—in a ten-game set, 6-4. I will never know how I survived those matches, perhaps by sheer luck, or Sue got bored returning my steady, but always-the-same forehand, and started thinking about dinner.

We shook hands as we walked off the court. Glancing over our shoulders at the boys still practicing on the real courts, we mused, "Maybe it will rain next week."

At the end of that season, I quit tennis.

❊ ❊ ❊

"Last call for pancakes," I offered one last opportunity to a not-quite-awake crowd of nervous—mostly, seventeen-year-old—girls slumped around our kitchen table and sprawled across the sofa in the adjoining family room. I struggled myself—to stay awake—and stifled a yawn. It was still dark outside, but I noticed hopeful hues of pink radiating through a charcoal sky as the first rays of a rare October sun crept through Douglas firs around our northwest home.

"More orange juice? Bacon? There's plenty."

"Thanks a lot, but I'm full," they murmured and pushed their plates away.

They buried their heads into SAT practice booklets, readying themselves to take the dreaded Scholastic Aptitude Test—the over-rated, but required pre-college exam—to determine which tier of colleges and universities might offer them entrance.

I had known these girls—now, in their senior year of high school—since they attended elementary and middle schools together. I volunteered as a room mother—the mom who iced their names on frosted surfaces of giant, heart-shaped cookies. I rooted for them at spelling bees as they fidgeted on the stages of vast school auditoriums. I endured spring drizzles and cheered at field days, track meets, and softball games, as they sprinted across playfields, their hair flying in the wind. I drove them—seat-belted, in carpools—to ballet, piano lessons, confirmation, summer camps, and birthday parties. Now I was prepared to escort them to SAT testing before they scattered across the country.

A few days earlier, my daughter begged, "Mom, is there any chance a few of my friends could spend the night before we take the SAT?"

I gasped, "Are you kidding me? This isn't a good night for a slumber party. This is serious stuff!"

"I know, but some parents can't get them to the test by 7:00 on Saturday morning. Jobs and other things going on."

I relented, "You know what? Sure. But lights out at ten, or else."

"Thanks, Mom." She raced to the phone to invite her friends.

I picked up the remaining dishes, as I scooted around the room, and broke the morning silence, "So, where are you planning to go to college?" A sudden chorus of shouts filled the air, "University of Washington, University of Puget Sound, Oregon, Montana State, Seattle University!"

Katie, a gifted athlete and honor student, looked up from filling-in-the-boxes, designed to advise the testing agency where to send her scores, and announced, "I want my results to only go to Lewis and Clark—you know—near Portland. I got a four-year scholarship to play basketball there. Then, I'm going to law school!"

"Wow! That's great. I'm so happy for you, Katie," I congratulated her, as I passed by, balancing the pile of dirty dishes.

Her eyes followed me. "Hey, Mrs. Kvinsland, did you play sports in high school?"

She caught me off guard. I stood still and mentally reached back almost thirty years.

"You know, Katie, I did. I played on the tennis team."

"Did you get a scholarship to college? To play tennis?" she asked.

I turned slowly and recalled softly, "No, not at all. In the 1960's, there were no athletic scholarships for girls. Only for boys."

Every head popped up from their practice pages, pens in hand. They gaped at me as if I had just announced that I had attended high school while serving time in prison.

"Are you kidding me? Really? I don't believe that!"

"Well, that's not fair!"

"How could that be?"

Now it was my turn for disbelief. A privileged generation sat before me, with no idea of what conditions had preceded the passing of the 1972 federal law that ended athletic discrimination in high schools and colleges. Even my daughter didn't know. Why hadn't I told her? Why didn't any of them know about struggling generations of girls and women born before them?

I glanced at the ticking clock and sighed, "Hurry up now. We need to leave in ten minutes."

This nerve-fraught day was probably not the best choice for their enlightenment. However, I couldn't help suggesting, as they piled into our well-used family Bronco, "Katie, when you get to law school, or hopefully, even sooner, can you look up Title IX?"

The sun crested the dense firs as I drove up our driveway. I glanced over my shoulder at their bright faces—and after a second thought—I added,

"You know, all of you need to do that. Soon. Okay?"

※ ※ ※

Last Saturday morning, my son texted me, "Ellie's game at 9:00. Steven's at 10. The park with the carousel."

The tiny letters on my iPhone provided my husband and I enough information to find the right location and ensure that we arrived in time for the opening day of spring soccer. Now, in our early seventies, we sometimes forgot timely details.

Shortly before nine, we pulled into the gigantic parking lot surrounding Southridge Sport and Events Complex. "Check your phone again. Did he say which field?" My husband wondered as we surveyed the mass of parked cars.

"No, but give me a minute," I hesitated, hoping to figure this maze out on our own, without bothering our son. I spotted his car parked several rows away. We hurried in that direction, our canvas chairs slung over our shoulders. As we scanned the nearby fields, our son's familiar purple cap—with UW embroidered in bold, white letters—shown above the crowd.

"Hey, Mom and Dad. Thanks for coming!" My son and his wife created space for us along the sideline. We unfolded our chairs and settled down to enjoy the morning.

"Wouldn't have missed it for anything," I replied, awed by the mass of tee-shirted five, six, and seven-year-olds mingling together on the fields. I scanned the expansive turf—recently spray painted with white boundary lines—and searched for my grandchildren.

I caught a glimpse of Ellie, surrounded by a familiar swarm of girls and boys. As I looked more closely, I recalled meeting a few of her coed teammates on Grandparents' Day in her first-grade classroom. Ellie broke away from her team and suddenly appeared before us. Lime green ribbons—chosen to match her tee-shirt—attempted to control her curly hair in twin ponytails, but errant strands were already struggling to free themselves from the ribbons' grip.

"Hi, LaLa," she smiled and paused long enough so I could hug her and reach into my pocket for my phone to snap her picture.

"Good luck," I shouted as she rushed back to her team for pre-game advice from her coaches, two, female soccer players from a nearby high school.

"Thud," the soccer ball soared above the soft grass after a rubber-cleated shoe made contact. Game on.

Parents yelled encouragement, "C'mon, Sam!" "Let's go, Alex!" Samantha and Alexandria brushed their fringed bangs out of their eyes, grinned confidently, and acknowledged the cheers. They blended into the herd of pounding feet as their team raced up and down the green turf.

I wondered about Steven, my grandson. I glanced away from Ellie's game and surveyed the adjacent fields until I found him sitting in a circle of preschool buddies who I recognized from his birthday parties: Haley, Myles, Aiden, Sara, Lisa, and Drew. I could pick out Steven's white socks in the circle—his favorites—the pair with Batman stamped upon the ribbed cotton.

On cue, the circle of matching shirts leaned over into Seated Forward Bends—noses touching knees, fingers reaching toes—warming up for their ten o'clock game, stretching their five-year-old hamstrings. When Katrina, their coach, led them into Downward-Facing-Dog—another yoga pose—I smiled and wished that I could join them.

I looked away, in time to see Ellie, playing goalie, spring up and bat away a potential score by the other team. Her teammates high-fived each other and dribbled the ball back upfield.

A tall man—standing near us—glanced over at my son and complimented him, "Nice hat!" He had paused to watch nearby play and deftly clutched a wiggly, toddler girl. We all looked toward them. We smiled when we noticed his cap was identical to my son's cap.

My son and the newcomer bantered back and forth above the din of the crowd, "Did you go to Washington? What year?"

We must have been eavesdropping because we all turned our heads when we heard the friendly stranger announce, "That's my wife over there in the red shirt. See her? She's coaching our son's team and refereeing games later today, too. She played soccer for Washington. Actually, she's the director of the whole Tri-Cities spring soccer program."

We stared and admired how deftly she sprinted along the sideline shouting encouragement to her team. Before we turned our attention to Ellie's game, we couldn't help but smile at the exhilarating action beside us.

I recall that my smile lasted for an unusually long time.

Part Two

Leaving: Uncharted Territory

6

No Way of Knowing

I had no way of knowing, as I reached for a piece of fried chicken, that I would never eat another delicacy like this, raised by my grandpa on his farm, at any future picnic. My Dad handed out crisp slices of watermelon—cooled in the icy Naches River—during our Memorial Day outing on Mount Rainier, while my mother scooped potato salad onto our paper plates. I had no way of knowing that the eggs in the potato salad would be the last dozen my grandpa would ever deliver to our home, or that the waxy, golden potatoes—the mainstay of the salad—would be the last ones he would dig out of his garden. I had no way of knowing that he was barely alive—felled by a massive stroke and robbed of his speech and mobility—until I saw my grandmother, forlorn and frail, clinging to their farmyard gate. "Grandpa's gone," she whispered, as we pulled up next to her. "He left in an ambulance, a few minutes ago." My family had dropped by on our way home from our picnic to bring them leftover chicken, potato salad, and a few slices of watermelon for their evening supper.

We will never know how many times grandma tried to call us, how many times the phone rang in our home that Memorial Day afternoon in the late 1950's. Answering machines, mobile phones, voicemail, texts, and email did not yet exist. My brothers and I stayed with my grandma as my parents sped off to the nearest hospital—nearly, one hour away—to check on grandpa's status.

We helped grandma into her living room chair and gently covered her with a ribbed afghan she had crocheted herself. Grandma was cold—unable to stop shaking—and sobbed quietly. I sat by her side and rubbed her arm. "It's going to be okay," I repeated again and again—fighting off my own tears, struggling to be brave. Both of us knew that *okay* was a condition we would not likely experience soon.

Grandma gazed at grandpa's velour rocker next to hers, his pipe and tobacco neatly displayed on the adjacent table. I knew where he kept his hard candies—lemon drops and raspberry-filled rounds—that he shared when our family gathered together to watch Milton Berle or Ed Sullivan, long before we could afford a television of our own. I refrained from reaching over and opening the tin box, although I wanted to. Maybe I should have opened it—passed the sugary treats around—and tried to create normalcy to ward off our fears.

My grandpa died a few months later, after a short stay in a nursing home. We had no way of knowing that grandma would be unable to live alone in the farmhouse they had shared for nearly fifty years. She tried, but the memories of their life there together haunted her. My mother called nightly—just before bedtime—to check on her well being.

Sometimes, as I drifted off to sleep, my mother whispered in my ear, "I'm making you a bed on the couch. Dad drove up to get Grandma. She'll sleep in your bed."

I never questioned or complained about Grandma's sleepovers. I loved her dearly. She loved me unconditionally. During my childhood, she had soothed my pain as she bandaged up my cuts and bruises, baked and cooked all of my favorites, never missed my birthdays or school concerts, and patiently listened to my awkward attempts to play the piano and accordion, even paying for my lessons.

I had no way of knowing that after a number of these evenings during my first year of high school, Grandma would move permanently into our home. One afternoon I found a canvas cot—a military leftover from a surplus store—squeezed into my tiny bedroom. I stormed into the kitchen, looking for my mother, who'd simply didn't have the energy to discuss the change with me. She was deeply stressed and exhausted herself.

I stomped around. "Please, this just isn't fair. I can't share my room. How can I have a slumber party without my own room?" I was belligerent. Even if I was later surprised by my selfish outrage—putting myself above my grandmother's pain—my mother was appalled by my thoughtless pleading. Through clenched teeth, she reminded me, "We have no choice. We have to help her, so be quiet. Go make room in your closet and drawers for grandma's things. The cot is yours."

I had no way of knowing—until we shared my tiny room—how deeply grandma was grieving. I laid awake most nights listening to her sob, muttering muffled phrases spoken in Norwegian, her native language. One morning, I asked her what she was said in the middle of the night.

She gazed at me sadly, and apologized, "I'm so sorry to be here. I am praying to die. I want to join your grandpa. I don't want to live any longer." Shocked by her words, I managed to console her, "Please don't die, grandma. We need you here with us. We love you." We clung to each other, and over time, her nightly anguish, and mine subsided.

❊❊❊

We had no way of knowing that Grandma would grow stronger during that long year, capable of living on her own again. My parents found her a small, over-the-water apartment—built on a dock above Puget Sound—in the tiny village of Annapolis, across from Bremerton and the naval shipyard.

Grandma's short time in Annapolis was very satisfying for her. She presided over her own kitchen again, baked bread, lemon-raisin cookies, and traditional Norwegian fattigman, sandbakels, and lefse. Before her farm was sold, my parents moved her favorite chair and her Motorola television into the tiny living room so she could enjoy *The Ed Sullivan Show* on Sunday nights. They placed her pale green, painted wooden table and chairs in the kitchen so she and my mother could visit and drink coffee together, nearly every weekday morning.

I had no way of knowing that her short stay in Annapolis would become so significant for me. I was a cheerleader and needed to practice after school on Mondays and Wednesdays, as well as return to campus at 5:30 every Tuesday and Friday—game nights at South Kitsap High School. Everyone agreed that I should stay with grandma on practice days and game nights since we only had one car that my dad needed for work. I had no transportation to go back and forth.

I was thrilled. It was a magical time for me. I became a city girl, a townie in Annapolis, which was not much of a town, but certainly more exciting than Harper.

On game nights, after I had dinner with grandma and finished my homework, I hiked up the hill—back to the high school—collecting my girlfriends, some of whom were cheerleaders like me. I knocked on the doors of their child-filled homes that lined the street between grandma's apartment and the high school. We were all juniors and seniors—giggling and dreaming of our futures—as we trekked in the growing darkness, carrying heavy metal flashlights that our dads insisted that we carry.

I don't recall if grandma knew about curfews. If she did, she didn't bother me with them during the year we roomed together off and on in Annapolis. I always caught a ride back home to her apartment with my boyfriend, who was the quarterback of the football team and a starting forward on the basketball team. I came in much later than I normally did—when I was subject to the scrutiny of my parents' watchful eyes. I crept quietly into the bed that grandma had made for me on her couch.

I was away at college when grandma slipped in the bathtub and broke her hip. That tragic accident activated a series of moves into assisted living spaces, accompanied by decreased mobility, that she bravely endured for the rest of her life.

For a short time in Annapolis, grandma and I practiced independence together; grandma, nearing eighty, a reluctant widow, learning to live on her own. I was a teenager, away from my parents, trying out freedom, trying to manage it wisely, with the hope of more to come.

❊❊❊

During my cash-strapped freshman year of college, I saved up small foil containers of sugary spreads from the condiment dispenser in the student dining room. When I returned home on breaks, I always brought grandma a brown paper sack stuffed with Smucker's marmalade, grape jelly, and strawberry jam. I had no way of knowing how eagerly she awaited these simple gifts.

Later, when my fortune improved, I gave her clean, unwrinkled, one-dollar bills—as many as I could afford—for her birthdays, Christmas, and Mothers' Day. Her tidy Norwegian sensibility did not tolerate well-worn, well-used money that had passed from one dirty hand to another. Intent upon pleasing her, I always walked into a bank to trade in my weathered bills for new, bright green replacements—smooth, new dollars—for her gifts.

Grandma died in 1967. Shortly after her death, one of my aunts sadly gathered up grandma's personal items—left behind in a single dresser drawer—in a nursing home in Seattle.

My aunt was shocked to discover all of the greetings cards that I had given grandma, stacked together neatly in her large pocketbook. I had no way of knowing that the money was unspent. I had no way of knowing that every crisp dollar bill was still inside each card—the envelopes addressed, "To Grandma," all of them signed, "Love, Judy." I was heartbroken. I had imagined that my small gifts had eased the challenge of a meager Social Security check that was her sole income during the final years of her life.

My aunt gathered up the cards and their contents, stuffed them into a large Manila envelope, and mailed the stash back to me. I gave the money to the building fund of a nearby Lutheran church. Grandma's gifts—along with other memorial gifts—funded stained glass windows in the sanctuary, which gave me comfort, whenever I attended services there.

I didn't need grandma's unexpected gift. She had already given me the most important gifts of my lifetime—unconditional love, gentle understanding, undivided attention, and continuous praise for my childhood efforts, whether deserved or not.

I had no way of knowing that grandma's kind and beautiful soul would compel me to name my own daughter, Anna-Louise, in her honor. I had no way of knowing—more than fifty years after her death—how often I would think of her, as I follow in her footsteps, now a grandma myself.

7

Best-laid Plans

I panicked near the end of my first semester of college when I realized that my scrimping and saving were not enough to cover costs of spring semester. I was broke.

Feeling desperate, I needed to talk to someone and share my dilemma. Maybe someone—more experienced with college costs—would know more than me, the first person in my family to attend college. My kind, usually-wise roommate took a break from her textbook and afternoon studies. She was an only child, the pride of her family, and from my vantage point, didn't seem to have too many cares. She listened carefully as I explained my predicament, then suggested, "Oh, just call your parents. That's what I'd do. Really, it's no big deal."

It was a big deal. I was the eldest of four kids, from a working-class family, attending a private university. I was not a legacy student—whose parents had attended this university—like many students I had met.

Those families had been saving for this experience and anticipating college costs for many years.

Economically, my family's needs were always met, but the totality of college expenses was new to us, especially the additional costs of textbooks, course fees for materials and supplies, and money needed for extras; laundry, food on weekends when the cafeteria closed, and other unknowns we had overlooked. These unexpected costs had slowly drained away the money I had saved for my second semester. I came up short.

I had never discussed finances with my high school advisors. I had never discussed finances with my college advisor. Money and family finances were generally viewed as matters of privacy in the early 1960's.

"Thanks," I replied weakly and decided to take a walk, hoping for a miracle to solve my problem. I recalled the image of my parents and myself—hovered over our kitchen table last spring—plotting my college future. After we pored over the estimated fees for tuition, room and board, my dad sharpened a pencil using the jackknife he always carried in his pocket. He made a few furtive calculations on the back of my mom's grocery list which was handy and within his reach. I waited expectantly. After a while, dad looked at his string of numbers, carefully printed a dollar figure on the back of mom's list, and proudly pushed it across the table to me. I noticed immediately that his figure was only enough for one semester of tuition, room and board. Undaunted, I accepted his tentative promissory note.

I was hopeful. I was grateful. "Thanks, mom and dad for your help. Don't worry. I'm saving every dollar I make now. I'll get a summer job, and save all of my earnings to carry me through the second semester."

My naïveté was unparalleled.

I meandered across the campus that late fall afternoon—kicking fallen leaves out of my path—and thought about my roommate's hollow suggestion. I knew I could not call my parents and ask for any more money. They had nothing more to give me.

My troubled walk took me past the On-Campus Jobs Board, nailed to the kiosk, in front of the Office of Student Services. Only one, on-campus job remained open for spring semester, actually, in my own dormitory:

Janitorial Assistant, North Hall. Duties to include: Dry dusting and wet mopping of all second-floor hallways and bathrooms. Hours of work: Monday-Friday, 3:00 to 5:30 A.M. Applicant must be dependable, able to work independently with little/no supervision, able to lift heavy buckets, industrial mops, and equipment. Trustworthy.

I sobbed in the pre-dawn silence on my first day at work until I had no more tears left inside of me. My self-esteem took a deep dive, assailed by an inner conversation I was having with myself; Is this what I am really destined to be? A part-time janitor? Am I over my head here at this college, even though I had been admitted with Honors at Entrance? How could this have happened? Didn't I save every dollar I had earned during the past year? Didn't I check my ledger every single morning to track my spending? I was humiliated.

With all of the strength that I could muster from my then one-hundred-pound frame, I bent down and hoisted the heavy, dripping mop out of its soapy bucket. I sloshed a steady pathway around the halls of my darkened dormitory, quietly mopping past the closed doors of my roommate and friends as they peacefully slept.

I was alone. I was the only person awake on my floor, long before dawn. As I began to get the feel for that dreaded mop, I began to strategize. How could I be the first person in line at the end of the next semester, on the exact day when student jobs became available?

Not only did I secure an easier, daytime work-study job for the next semester, but I dug deeper. I learned about financial aid and secured a student loan created by the National Defense Education Act (NDEA) Student Loan program, designed to support students who wanted to be teachers, like myself. I shared this information with my brothers and sister who followed behind me, all of us supported by student loans, that we appreciated and repaid. I was the last janitor in my family.

8

A Day, Unlike Any Other

I stood steadfast. I struggled to remain calm. I was close enough to President John F. Kennedy to make eye contact, close enough for him to smile and nod at me, close enough for me to realize that if I did something rash—like reach out to shake his hand—I could be whisked away by the Secret Service or, even worse, pin-pointed in the scope of one of the uniformed sharpshooters stationed above me on the roof of Cheney Stadium. It was September 27, 1963, a day, unlike any other.

Just last week, the President of my university summoned me to his office, without giving me any agenda for the meeting. We had met during freshman orientation. We exchanged brief greetings whenever we passed each other on campus. He had sent me a congratulatory form letter last spring when I was selected for membership in a sophomore women's honorary. He sent another short personal note when I was elected president of that group. As I rushed toward the administration building, I couldn't imagine any reason he would want to talk to me. I even wondered if I had done something wrong.

"I have been notified that President Kennedy will make a stop here in Tacoma next week during the last leg of his conservation tour of the western states. Dr. Thompson, the president of the University of Puget Sound, and I are arranging a joint convocation for the faculty and students of our universities. We've been asked by the advance planners for President Kennedy's visit to select five students from each campus to form an Honor Guard to welcome the President. They will be the first point of contact once his helicopter lands. I would like you to be one of our university's representatives," he explained.

I gaped at Dr. Mortvedt in disbelief. President Kennedy was my hero. Like many others in my generation, I was inspired by his leadership. I pored over his speeches in the newspaper and looked for glimpses of him on television, always motivated and energized by his thoughts and ideas.

For a moment, I stood speechless, unable to grasp the opportunity before me. I was in shock. At last, I found my voice, "Yes. Oh, yes. For sure!"

I found a payphone and called my mother. I jumped up and down in the booth, as students passed by me, wondering what had just happened, why I was so excited. My mother, a life-long Democrat, cried with joy. My father, a life-long Republican, called me later after work, thrilled and extremely proud. I was going to meet the President of the United States—something unimaginable to us. The next morning, the Secret Service requested the Social Security numbers of my parents and myself, to ensure that there were no unfavorable issues in our past.

It seemed that I had to gain security clearance to be near the President. Fortunately, we passed their scrutiny.

Before dawn, on the morning of the President's visit, I huddled alongside other members of the Student Honor Guard in Cheney Stadium. Fit and trim members of the crew-cut Secret Service drilled us on expected behavior. Where to stand. How to stand. What to do, what not to do: "Keep your cool. Just smile. Look alive. Stay calm." I glanced up at the sharpshooters lining the rooftop of the stadium and shivered after they cautioned us, "No sudden moves." For a brief moment, I doubted whether this honor was a good idea, but I swiftly recovered.

It wasn't long before thousands of students, faculty, and staff—nearly the entire campus communities of both universities—filled the bleachers behind us. The air was electric. The din of the crowd soared when we heard the rhythmical clickety-clack of the rotary blades of the President's helicopter approach the stadium, long before we could see it. The military helicopter—from nearby Fort Lewis—burst through the few wispy clouds that remained in the bluebird sky and dropped to the pavement before me.

Instantly, the young President appeared at the door of the Army helicopter emblazoned with the Seal of the Presidency. He raised his hand in greeting. A roar rose up from the bleachers, louder, more exciting, more passionate than anything I had ever heard at a sporting event or a concert. I fought back my desire to jump up and down, to scream and clap along with the crowd, but I remembered that the Secret Service had their eyes on me, as well as the President. I kept my cool.

President Kennedy lightly skipped down the steps of the helicopter.

Within seconds, he stood in front of me. He nodded and flashed his wide smile at me, as he walked by, and repeated that action with every other student as he worked his way through the receiving line. My eyes remained riveted on him, as he nonchalantly brushed his wayward, thick auburn hair away from his forehead. He appeared relaxed, but fumbled now and then with the button on his single-button grey suit, as if to give his hands something to do, since he couldn't shake ours. When he reached the speaker's platform—temporarily constructed over the pitcher's mound in front of the bleachers—he turned and grinned at the students, faculty, and staff screaming in the bleachers.

I did not think it was possible, but their exhilaration increased in volume, cresting like a wave, as the President approached the podium and prepared to speak. The roar of the crowd became deafening.

To the chagrin of the traveling press corps, once the President realized that his audience was so young, he cast aside his formal, prepared remarks about conservation and launched into a different address, different than the press release they had been issued. The press corps—who stood behind us—grumbled and complained, "What's he doing? What's going on?" Annoyed, and likely exhausted themselves—nearing the end of a ten-day trip—they took out their notebooks and started jotting down highlights of his new speech, prepared to file new stories.

The President spoke extemporaneously and delivered his message, seemingly, just for us, on the brink of our futures:

"Senators Magnuson and Jackson, Governor Rossellini, Secretary of the Interior Udall, University Presidents Mortvedt and Thompson, my fellow citizens, and especially to you, the students and faculty of these two fine universities:

"....Nothing is more important today than for us to realize how an educated citizenry can assist in solving the challenges of a country.

…..Those of you, who are now in school, will prepare yourselves to bear the burden of leadership over the next forty years, here in the United States, to make sure that the United States…which I believe almost alone has maintained watch and ward for freedom…that the United States meet its responsibility." (John F. Kennedy Presidential Library and Museum. Folder Title: Remarks at Cheney Stadium, Tacoma Washington, 27 September 1963).

Thanksgiving that year was somber. Christmas was not much better. Before I returned to college after Christmas break, my mother handed me a copy of The Torch is Passed, a collection of stories, recently compiled by members of The Associated Press, some of whom were in Cheney Stadium that September day. "Don't ever forget," she said. I haven't. I still pull the book from one of my bookshelves and turn to the foreword….."This chronicle is written, not to revive shock and tears, but to remember"

9

The Question

Before my maid of honor left the tiny anteroom—reserved for bridal parties—on my wedding day at Our Saviour's Lutheran Church, she glanced over her shoulder and smiled. "See you soon," she mouthed. "You bet," I whispered back. Nancy and I knew each other well. We had lived together for the past two years as college roommates.

Now my dad and I were alone. Dad was a handsome man, blue-eyed, with hair, still jet black, even though he was nearing fifty. He had a rugged complexion, deeply tanned, by rays of the sun that reflected off the deck of the tugboat he captained on Puget Sound. He ran his work-worn fingers around the inside collar of the stiff white shirt that accompanied his rented tuxedo. He tugged at its starched surface. He seemed fidgety and uncomfortable as if he was searching for air. The day was unbearably hot—rare, for Puget Sound summers. The tiny room had been overheated by the presence of five bridesmaids, who had disappeared one by one before Nancy also floated away.

Nancy must have reached the altar because I could hear the final strains of Bach's, "Jesu, Joy of Man's Desiring," quietly fade. Bach was new to me—absent in my childhood home—but joyfully discovered in Music 101 at college. I was more familiar with Wagner's "Bridal Chorus," since many of my college friends had married earlier that summer. They sat in the pews of the white clapboard church, along with the families and other friends of the groom and myself.

I heard the organist transition into the opening notes of the "Bridal Chorus." I glanced over my shoulder at the long train of my wedding gown, a dress that Best's Apparel—later known as Nordstrom-Best, and then just Nordstrom's—had described as "Fashioned of white satin with an empire bodice of Alencon lace with scallops of lace edging the Sabrina neckline and elbow-length sleeves." I felt wonderful. I was eager to join my groom.

We took a few steps toward the door that led to the aisle. Suddenly, my dad stopped and said, "I need to ask you something."

Surprised, I stared at him.

"Is this what you want to do right now? More than anything else in the world? Is getting married what you really want to do?"

I was stunned. "Dad, what are you talking about. Of course, it is. You know I love Steve. Yes, I want to marry him!"

"Because if it isn't, we'll walk right out that door over there together." He gestured, away from the aisle, toward the open doors that led to the street outside. "I'll go with you. No questions asked."

I was aghast. I was hurt. Where was this inquiry coming from? Steve and I had dated through high school and college. We loved each other.

We had never shown a moment of hesitation.

"Dad, I want to marry Steve. More than anything else in the world."

Dad relaxed. He took a deep breath. He patted my kid-gloved hand that was slipped through the crook of his left elbow.

"Well, then. Let's go!"

The organist peered over the heads of our three hundred guests and saw dad and I smiling, standing there together, herself, unaware of the discussion behind us. She saw that we were ready to take our first steps down the white-carpeted aisle. She adjusted the row of stops on the organ and majestically played the "Bridal Chorus."

I still wonder if dad was thinking about my marriage that day, or if he was thinking about his own life. Shortly after my wedding, the marriage of my parents began to unravel. Was he trying to caution me, or was he thinking about his own impending difficulties, wishing life had been different? As close as my dad and I were, we never mentioned that moment again.

10

Uncharted Territory

On the day that my father turned fifty-nine, our lives crashed down around us. His early July birthday coincided with the departure of overcast, drizzly skies that Puget Sounders endured during rainy springs in the Pacific Northwest. Summer often arrived late—sunny and bright—around his birthday and lured us outside to resume familiar pleasures on the water and beaches again. That day was no exception. At least, the weather was no exception.

My parents' driveway was long and provided visitors enough lag time, while driving up the rutted road, "to get the lay of the land," as my father liked to say. What's in bloom? What needs work? Who's outside? What's going on? As my family and I crested the familiar hill in our car stuffed with food and birthday gifts, I saw dad standing still, gazing off into the distance. We honked. I waved at him, but he looked away and seemed oblivious of our arrival as if frozen in place.

He wasn't bustling about with his outdoor broom, sweeping up prickly, fallen cedar needles that littered the driveway. He wasn't bent over a stubborn dandelion, struggling to yank it out of his carefully tended vegetable garden next to the driveway. He didn't even have a pressure gauge stuffed into his back pocket. Dad had a habit of checking the tire pressure of every car that brought visitors. He never stopped caring about our welfare and safety.

I got out of the car and placed his birthday cake—that I had held on my lap for nearly an hour—on the seat behind me. Dad stood silent—almost trance-like—and stared at me. I walked toward him and waited for his usual and customary greeting:

"Well, what-do-you-know, if it isn't my firstborn, that little girl, who they told me was a boy. I never cared about that mix-up one bit. I tell ya, I've never minded it at all." Dad loved to retell the story of my wartime birth when the Red Cross notified him by telegram, "You have a son." Jubilation must have reigned in Fort Wheeler, Georgia. Mom's telegram arrived a few days later, "I named her Judith Louise." Dad never missed a chance to laugh about that mixed-up event.

Today, there was only silence.

I spoke first, "Hi Dad! Happy Birthday!" I embraced him tightly.

The wind rustled through the cedar trees, the only sound I could hear.

I continued, "Where's Mom? Are you okay? Is everything alright?"

He shrank from my hold and remained silent. He seemed relieved—almost thankful—to be released from my annual birthday hug.

With his head down, he finally mumbled, "She's in the house. You better go check on her."

※※※

I found my mother in the living room, sunk into her favorite recliner—flattened against the tufted beige—as if the wind had been knocked out of her. She wept softly, continuously, like a person who had been grieving and mourning for quite some time. A steady—seemingly, endless—stream of tears poured from her swollen, reddened eyes. The front of her faded pink chenille robe—the one she reached for each morning when she arose to make coffee—was wet, actually drenched.

I sat down next to her and asked over and over, "Mom, what's wrong?" My questions accelerated her weeping. I quit asking.

I looked around in search of a clue. The living room looked mostly the same. The bookshelf behind her recliner revealed the spines of all of The Little Golden Books and classic novels that she had bought for us. My favorites peeked out next to her cookbooks—Betty Crocker and Better Homes and Gardens, her gurus. The shelves needed dusting, which was unusual since mom's housekeeping was impeccable.

The morning sun had already abandoned the east-facing living room—left it behind—and was traveling southward, where it would eventually burst into the adjacent dining room, later in the day. Right now, the room was dark and in need of light.

I opened the living room door, desperate to brighten up the familiar space which was small and compact, but felt smaller, tighter and more confining at this moment—even claustrophobic. Once I opened the door, light flowed in, along with salty air from Puget Sound, in front of the house.

I made Mom a cup of steaming, instant coffee. She was the only person I knew who would drink that poor-excuse-for-a-cup-of-coffee.

I handed Mom her favorite mug that I had bought her at The Kennedy Library in Boston. I noticed the gilt inscription, "There are three things which are real: God, Human Folly, and Laughter. The first two are beyond our comprehension. So we must do what we can with the third—John F. Kennedy." There was no laughter in this room.

After the caffeine jolt, Mom momentarily calmed down. I tried again, "Mom, what's wrong. What's going on?" I patted her shoulder gently and tried to comfort her.

Her torrent of tears began anew. "Go, ask your dad," she moaned.

I retraced my steps through the house, back to the driveway where my confused family waited patiently, and my father held his ground.

"Dad, what is going on here," I demanded.

"I just don't want to be here anymore," he sighed. This time, he looked directly into my widened blue eyes—a hue that I had inherited from both of my parents—and reiterated, "I don't want to live here with your mother anymore."

❊ ❊ ❊

My parents separated after nearly thirty-five years together. Dad moved on, into a new relationship, and left mom behind—saddened, forlorn, and often unmoored—in the family home. Oddly, they never divorced, but remained separated, for the rest of their lives. It was a rare occasion that found my parents in the same room again—reuniting only for the weddings of my youngest brother and sister. My father divided his wages in half, maintained her health insurance, and legally arranged for her to receive his retirement funds, ensuring that mom was able to—at least—live economically comfortable.

Their life-long separation required me and my siblings to create new ways to be with our parents—individually, separately—to celebrate holidays, birthdays and family events. We organized and hosted two celebrations for every occasion. Christmas on one day with mom. Christmas on a different day with dad. As challenging as it was, we managed to remain close to both of our parents for the rest of their lives.

It took me a long time to get over the gravity of dad's announcement, "I just don't want to be here anymore." The moment haunted me. I dropped into an abyss. Unfortunately, I miscarried the child that I was carrying, and endured a depression that paralyzed me, left me helpless. I put on a brave front for my children, continued to teach part-time, and trudged through my days the best that I could. Fortunately, with the love and support of my husband—along with friends and colleagues who understood the depth of my pain—I was able to stabilize, pull myself out of the doldrums and resume my life, which gradually took a positive turn. I went back to graduate school, earned another degree, quit teaching to become a college administrator, and moved steadily up the career ladder.

There was a price. Unmoored by my parents' separation, devastated by grief, saddened by the loss of a pregnancy—followed by deep depression—I learned to protect myself emotionally. I did not allow myself to fully feel sadness when disappointments came my way. I created an emotional survival zone, a neutral way of living, so I would never be as vulnerable to disasters as I was when my parents separated. There was a cost to my primitive means of survival. Just as I was able to routinely shake off disappointments, I didn't allow myself to fully experience joy. I knew through experience, that happiness could also be torn away in an instant. I lived in an emotionally-neutral, protective state of being, until one day, I no longer could.

❊ ❊ ❊

After I conducted the annual faculty and staff orientation on the first day of the fall quarter in 2003, I returned to my office, exhausted and worn. My sister and I had sat up all night with my mother in the emergency room of a nearby hospital, keenly aware that she was no longer able to live independently. Mom's health and mobility were failing rapidly. We needed to find her more help and a new place to live.

I sat at my desk, paged through my calendar, and began to rearrange meetings and commitments, looking for time to canvas the community and find mom a new home, and hopefully, help her relocate. I was overwhelmed and over-scheduled already, and the academic year had just begun. I idly flipped through the calendar, wondering if I needed to take a leave of absence, until I reached the page for November. I stared at the bold, solid line drawn through the first week of the month. I stared at my handwriting, "Out of the Office." For a moment, I was confused—caught off guard—probably, from the lack of sleep the night before. I couldn't seem to grasp or remember why this week was important. Then I remembered: I was going to California for the birth of our first grandchild. How could I have forgotten? How could I have overlooked this happy, anticipatory event in my life? At that moment, I was broken. All I could think of was, "One more thing to fit in. One more thing I have to do." I needed help. I had reached my limits.

❊ ❊ ❊

I hesitated a week later, when a therapist—recommended by a

friend—asked me, "Why are you here? What made you schedule this appointment today?"

I was silent at first. I stared down at my hands, clenched in my lap. I looked up, avoided her gaze, and let my eyes wander around her comfortable office that I had already studied before she walked in. I reached for a tissue on the low table between us and dabbed at tears that started to drip down my cheeks.

"I want my joy back. I remember what it's like to be joyful. I can't seem to feel any joy right now. I have many reasons to be happy, but I can't hold on to those feelings. Sadness creeps in over the top of them. I want my joy back."

Six weeks later, after confronting excruciating moments that had caused me to protect myself emotionally, I felt free. I felt alive again. I learned that I could grieve, feel losses, and lift myself. That was life. I learned that I could celebrate, be fully joyful in the moment, and not agonize that it could all be taken away. I trusted in my resilience, something that I had lost, but with the help of a therapist, I found it again. I'm sorry I waited so long.

"Send me a picture of your grandchild," the therapist said, as we hugged each other before I left for California. I did. I never saw her again.

Part Three

Changes: Disturbing the Calm

11

Disturbing the Calm

After more than thirty years of active parenting, our nest in Gig Harbor was finally empty. I no longer needed to make frantic calls from the road to check on my children's welfare because traffic on the Narrows Bridge was backed up. If I needed to work late, I did. After work, my husband and I met for dinner. Our favorite restaurants entered into our conversations again, "The Lobster Shop or Marzano's, tonight?" We enjoyed the movies after dinner. We often ran an errand or two. The Bridge was traffic-free and free-flowing by the time we crossed. When we returned home, our house looked just like we had left it that morning. No more backpacks, textbooks, or running shoes in the entry. No cereal bowls stacked in the sink. We had happily adjusted and were enjoying our new lifestyle. Grandparenting could wait.

Or at least I thought so, three years into our empty nesting, when our daughter announced her first pregnancy. I was busily clearing off my desk at the college where I worked—anticipating a weekend of well-deserved relaxation—when the phone rang.

"Hi, Mom," chirped Anna, now eight hundred miles away in northern California.

"Hi there, Sis," I reverted to our family's term of endearment.

She continued, "Sorry to be so late in calling, Mom, but could you fly down and go with me to my first midwife appointment? It's on Monday."

"*This* Monday," she clarified. I'd feel a lot better if you could be here with me. Please, Mom?"

I began to formulate an excuse. *What was she thinking?* Didn't she realize that I had next week's workload already planned? I'm swamped here.

But I quickly changed my tune. *What was I thinking?* My only daughter had invited me to participate in one of life's most intimate moments. I slashed a bold line through my calendar to block out the upcoming week, dialed Alaska Airlines, and booked a flight to Oakland.

Three days later—comfortably seated in a bright, sun-lit room at Caring For Women, a health clinic in Fort Bragg—I leaned closer to the examination table that held my daughter. The mid-wife was carefully maneuvering the ultrasound machine closer to her, preparing to scan Anna's just-beginning-to-round belly.

"Just a warning. This will be cold at first," the mid-wife cautioned. She gently smoothed the icy conductive gel into a widening circle, followed by the flattened scope, round and round the barely noticeable baby bump. Anna flinched—as if on cue—but she quickly recovered, relaxed, and settled in for the exam. She gazed at me happily.

Suddenly, we heard, "Lub-dub, lub-dub, lub-dub." My eyes swelled with tears.

"Lub-dub, lub-dub. I'm here, I'm here," a heartbeat, like an unknown voice, fluttered about and filled the tiny room. I was not prepared to be as smitten by the faint presence who had just introduced itself to us. My heart was captivated.

Afterward, we drove cautiously down Redwood Avenue on our way back to her home in Mendocino, both keenly aware of the important cargo on board. The afternoon sun reflected off the Pacific with enough glare that forced us to lower the windshield visors to dispel the sparkle of the ocean and dazzle of the day.

"Hey Mom, did you know that there's a nice little college over there?" Anna announced. She momentarily released her right hand from the wheel, thrust her arm before me, and pointed toward the ocean's edge.

She laughingly proposed, "You should get a job there so you can be here when the baby is born!"

I rolled the window down so I could see better. As I peered toward the horizon, I could hear the waves crashing before me. Through the bright curtain of sun and ocean mist, I could just barely make out the shapes of several sprawling buildings with reddish-brown roofs that rose slightly above the jagged edge of the cliff. The appealing little campus was surrounded by open fields of golden grass, that waved in the ocean breeze. Distinct rows of California cypress trees—with grey-green foliage, shaped into abstract sculptures by the prevailing westerly winds—neatly defined the campus boundaries.

"I already have a job. It's not as if I need another one."

I began to visualize myself as a frequent flier: Seattle-to-Oakland, Oakland-to-Seattle. Work-weeks-in-Washington. Grand parenting-

Weekends-in-California.

But, I couldn't stop thinking about her proposal. It became one of those recurrent can't-get-it-out-of-my-mind thoughts. A new, internal voice began to resonate within me,

"Why not? Why not? Why not?"

Soon another faint, familiar voice joined in,

"Lub-dub, lub-dub. I'm here, I'm here."

Both voices danced their way through my mind for the remainder of the afternoon. By the time I called my husband that evening to relate the highlights of the day, possibilities had permanently dug in, prepared to grab hold of our destiny.

"Tell me about your day," he said.

"It was great. I'm moving to California!" I announced with unabashed confidence and commitment.

I was not surprised by my declaration. Clearly, he was.

His voice wavered a bit, "Will I be coming along too?"

"I hope so," I blurted out.

He had just retired and my retirement was not too far away. We had paid off our house. We were downsizing. An unplanned adventure like this had not been part of our budget plans. He was also familiar with what we called, "Judy's Hair-brained Ideas," a concoction of thoughts and dreams I often harbored and carried around. After I processed them for a while, I usually cast them aside and moved on.

Not this time.

After a long silence, he wondered, "Will we be able to eat?"

Now he had me. I wasn't quite ready to disclose that during my afternoon of imagined possibilities, I had visited the local college's website and learned that a new position was about to open on their campus, similar to the position I held in Washington.

I swallowed hard and attempted to console him, "I don't know that yet, but I am going to work on it."

He sighed, "Well, we don't owe any more college tuition. We paid off the orthodontist long ago, and our last pet has died. I think we have a slight window of opportunity here."

The next few months flashed by, filled with a flurry of activities: I applied for the new job at the college in Fort Bragg; survived a three-day, grueling interview process; accepted the job offer; signed a two-year, renewable contract; leased a rental home, sight unseen; filled a small rented van with a few essentials to begin our new life; and locked the door of our long-time family home behind us.

Most evenings—after I returned from my workday at College of the Redwoods—we swaddled our infant granddaughter into her stroller and sauntered down the hill to the village of Mendocino, to marvel at the sun setting below the horizon of the Pacific Ocean—just minutes away from our new home.

We never looked back.

12

A Reason for Flight

I slid my driver's license across the counter and checked in for my flight back to California. I was alone. My family stayed behind at our beach house on Puget Sound for the last few days of summer. I needed to return to my new job at College of the Redwoods. The ticketing agent's fingers tapped across the keyboard. Without a glance, she announced, "I need you to relocate. A family needs your seat, so they can sit together." Before I could react, her printer forecasted my future—already shaky—on the saddest day of my life.

"How about first class? Will that work?" She handed me a new boarding pass. I dragged myself aboard Alaska's final, Seattle-to-Oakland flight of the day. I hunkered down in my leather cubicle and wished I could disappear. I needed to put this day behind me. A scraggly string of passengers passed by, peered down upon us in first class, eyeing, what we fortunate few had already been served.

Wearing their colors, exuberant alums of Washington and Cal taunted each other, exchanged high fives, and launched tentative bets on the upcoming football season. I accepted a glass of first-class champagne that was freely flowing.

I glanced over my shoulder and longed for my original seat—desperate for solitude, coach class anonymity, rows away from jubilation. I squeezed my eyelids together tightly and feigned sleep. After the plane reached its cruising altitude, flight attendants hovered, monitored my untouched flute of California bubbles—slowly dissipating—as I dozed and delved deeper into images from the day.

We buried my mother's ashes in a silver urn, atop the gravesite of her mother in the family plot in Sedgwick Cemetery. Like an archeological dig, funereal gurus made careful calculations, before her four adult children—her survivors—could honor her simple wish. "Yes, that will work," they said, after some discussion. "We haven't buried ashes before atop an existing grave, but if that's what you want, sure." We countered, "It is what she wanted. It was her wish." They allowed us to proceed.

Afterward, at a reception to celebrate my mother's life, her crones hugged, squeezed, and regaled me with their stories about her. Seventy-nine years in Kitsap county, my mother is remembered, even revered. A woman, who seemed vaguely familiar, approached, "Remember me? I'm Mae, from the Banner Birthday Club." We counted together—she and I—how many years had passed since we had last seen each other. Our tally reached fifty—fifty years since we had shared morsels of homemade, layered birthday cakes, tinted golden by the yokes of Rhode Island Reds, hens that free ranged in the chicken yards of my grandparents and their Norwegian neighbors.

"I remember you. You were the only mom who brought your bathing suit to the Birthday Club picnics at Long Lake. You were our lifeguard, willing to watch over us, swimming at our own risk. I think you even taught me to dive," I recalled. We hugged.

Like clockwork, the crowded Boeing 737 began its descent into Oakland. Cabin lights popped on. Voices stirred around me—invaded my tiny enclosure—and pulled me out of a troubled dream. Disoriented, I searched for a pencil. I tore a page from the in-flight magazine, jotted tasks down in the margins—broke ground on my weekly To-Do list. I needed to capture my thoughts before they escaped:

"Call Mom. Tell her about Mae."

It was at that moment—just then—that I began to grasp the reason for my flight.

13

The Promise

I dug among the Kleenex and grocery receipts stashed in the pocket of my hooded sweatshirt and searched for my chirping cell phone. I slid my forefinger across its glassy face and smiled when I heard Dad's voice float into my ear as he did every Saturday morning. Always early. Always the same greeting. Have you got a minute? Is this a good time?

He was not a man to engage in idle conversation. He never asked for more than was necessary or took more than he needed. He never infringed upon anyone or lost his gentle southern manners and grace.

I nestled down into a deck chair, outside on my patio with my favorite coffee cup. He had chosen the mug for me in a tourist shop when we traveled together one spring, on the Blue Ridge Parkway, in his native Virginia.

A mug, made in China. Spattered with pale pink mountain laurel, like the Virginia view before us. "Oh, that gift shop just needed some business," he apologized, as he smiled and self-consciously handed it to me.

We chugged through our list of mutual concerns that Saturday morning:

His garden, my garden.

His health, my health.

His travels, my travels.

His children, my siblings.

My grandchildren, his great-grandchildren, all of whom he called "Little Angels." Perhaps easier than remembering their names?

Dad paused. I sipped my coffee. The dark liquid was growing colder in the morning chill. I used his silence to admire the sunrise filtering through the California redwoods that towered over my home.

His voice broke through the momentary quiet, "I need you to do something for me," he said.

"Sure, Dad. What's up?"

There was another pause. I felt a growing concern about his well-being until I heard him stir about in his small sitting room. I realized that he was safe inside, protected from the spring squalls that gusted in from Puget Sound. I heard the creak of the glass door on his airtight stove as it swung open. I heard the steady thumping of his blackened stove poker as it pushed and prodded the pile of Douglas Fir around the firebox. I heard the snapping and crackling of the morning flames as the logs caught fire anew.

His extended silence raised my anxiety. I gently tried again, "What's up, Dad?"

"I need you to do something for me," he said, a second time. "If something happens to me, and I'm not conscious, I need you to decide about my life support. I named you in my advanced directive to make end-of-life decisions for me. If something happens to me….can you do that?"

My heart pounded in my ears. Tears dribbled from my eyes. The painful grief of my mother's recent death still followed me. "I can't do that, Dad," I said weakly. "I don't want to lose you. I just can't. Don't make me do that."

"You have to," he said. "You know, we might not be able to locate your brothers. Always out there in the wilderness, fishing or hunting. Somewhere out of cell range."

"And your sister. Well, you know your sister. She won't let me go. She'll keep me propped up in a hospital bed forever, like some god damned mummy, hooked up to machines. You've got to do this for me. You're the steady one. You know what matters to me in my life. The conditions that I need to keep on living, my way. Please?" Dad pleaded.

I felt his despair, his reluctance to have to ask for this kind of help.

"I will, Dad, I will. Don't worry," I mumbled through my sobbing.

We pulled ourselves together and exchanged our usual goodbyes:

"I love you, Dad."

"I love you too, a hundred times over."

One of us must have ended the call because suddenly I was alone in the morning silence. I sat frozen for a long time, grappling with the fear of losing another parent, feeling forlorn and frightened, wondering if I could fulfill my promise.

Now, there are days when I sit and hold his wrinkled, worn directive with my name on it in my hands. We found it in his wallet after he died, a few years later. A sudden death. An instant death. A massive coronary at the age of eighty-nine.

It's a reminder: I'm the steady one. The one who knows what matters in life. And even if I'm not that person, it reminds me that he believed I could be.

14

Doc Speak

My test results did not surprise me.

"Judy, I'm really sorry to have to tell you this, but the results of last week's biopsy indicate a malignancy. You will need surgery, possibly chemotherapy, perhaps even radiation," Dr. Allen disclosed after I answered the phone in my office.

Instantly, I recalled the team of nurses caring for me last week—one of them, my friend and neighbor—who avoided eye contact with me after I regained consciousness. Before the procedure, we commiserated about the summer fog, compared the progress of our gardens, and reveled in our experiences at the recent Mendocino Music Festival. I felt distance deepen between us as they cared for me, silently rolled me back to the recovery room, then back to my hospital room. They seemed glum—almost, saddened—as if they already knew something that I didn't, but would soon find out.

I was surprised that Dr. Allen had the empathy and grace to call me himself. I sat silently at my desk, trying to concentrate on his words. I grew numb. I could not speak. Only his optimism soothed me, "You will get through this. I've given you more information than you can process, more than you can deal with right now. I'll see you later this week in my office, and we can talk more. All I want you to take away from this conversation is, 'You will get through this. Just remember, you will get through this.'"

I didn't ever want to forget his hopefulness. Not then. Not soon.

I transformed his words into my personal mantra, "I will get through this. I will get through this." I was still reciting this litany—softly to myself, through clenched teeth—as I stepped into an oncologist's office in Santa Rosa, a week later—with his referral, clutched in my hands.

Soon I was perched upon a standard examination table, its worn, vinyl surface concealed by a stiff, sterile swath of white paper—the kind I used for finger painting years ago, during other summers. Barely covered, I pulled the edges of my flimsy tissue paper gown together. I began to shake and shiver from either the temperature or my anxiety, probably both.

No one consulted the mood-making, color stylists of Benjamin Moore before they painted that examination room. Stark white paint covered the cubicle; no soothing blue had been added to the mix to create calm or welcome. There was little on the walls to disturb the clinic's silent aura; oncology, we're serious here, so get ready. I continued to shake, wondering if my rustling was noticeable, with only tissue paper to disguise my nerves and fear.

The door swung open. I was greeted by a firm handshake, a no-

nonsense, take-no-prisoners kind of greeting.

"Hello, Judith. I'm Dr. Page, Beth Ann," she declared and looked straight into my eyes.

"Uh, it's Judy," I gasped, my shakes ramping up so significantly that I could observe a full tremor in my hand, as I withdrew it from hers. "How are you?"

"Well, you're the one I want to answer that question," she mused as she glanced down at my file in her other hand.

"I guess, I'm okay."

She reviewed my tests, interpreted them for me, one ominous statistic after another.

She continued, "Cancer is like this. We have about a ninety percent chance that we can get rid of this thing through surgery. Maybe with some additional chemo. Maybe with a regimen of radiation."

I sat there, desperate for something positive to cling to. Attempting to be brave and a little more in control, I surmised, "Well, those are pretty good odds. Maybe, I should go to Las Vegas as well?"

She smiled. I think I smiled too.

"It's the ten percent chance of what is *unknown* to us right now that I'm concerned about," she cautioned. "We won't know until we get in there if the cancer has spread to other organs. Now, if I find other areas impacted by cancer, and deem that surgical removal is necessary, do you want me to take care of it? Or do you want that taken care of at another time?"

"Uh, you're the expert, I don't know," I whispered.

I must have appeared delirious. I must have appeared out of my mind at her assumption that I had a well thought out opinion. I was out of my league here, out of my comfort zone.

"Please don't wake me up if you find something else, and make me do this again. Just fix it," I begged. My shivers and shakes intensified. My paper gown began to vibrate like a tuning fork.

With all of the courage and strength I could muster, I offered a plea, *"I just want to be cancer-free."*

She quietly rolled her padded stool up close to me. "We don't think in those terms. We're angling for a good outcome. You need to know that once a patient experiences cancer, they are at risk for that cancer to return, and their risk for other forms of cancer increases," she confided.

Downcast, I sat still for a while with nothing in the room to disturb the silence. Finally, I lifted my head, "Okay. I don't like that. I don't like that at all. But I get it."

"Well then, let's get this problem handled. Let's do this thing!" She stood up and embraced me while I quivered on the table. I clung to her tightly.

Three weeks later, following state-of-the-art, robotic surgery at UCSF at Mt. Zion Hospital, I awakened to voices, calling my name. My eyelids fluttered. I struggled to remain conscious to see who was there, my body, still heavily doped by anesthetics and pain medication.

"Ah, there you are," Dr. Page rejoiced. "Glad to have you back."

My husband stood beside her, smiling down at me, holding a massive bouquet of sunflowers in his arms.

Dr. Page held my hand and continued, "I have good news!"

I struggled to stay awake. I fought to focus on Dr. Page, who still wore her surgical garb, a large vinyl apron wrapped around her petite frame. I peered at the colorful assortment of cats and dogs, printed on the fabric of her once-sterile cap. A well-worn, heavy Patagonia fleece jacket was zipped up to her chin as if she was preparing for a mountain trek.

"We thought surgery would take us about three hours, but we needed almost five, to remove surrounding tissue and nodes, and wait for test results to come back from the lab. We're confident we got all of the cancer with this one surgery. No chemo needed. No radiation either."

I'm sure I smiled. I know I said thank you. My relief was overwhelming.

Before she left, she leaned down, close enough so I could hear her, "Now get yourself back to work, okay? Get back to that college. Get back out there and save the world!"

In the days and months that followed, I often thought about Dr. Page's charge. I worked for another year—oversaw the final renovations to my campus—and happily retired, after a thirty-five-year career. I danced with my son at his wedding. I welcomed three more grandchildren. My husband and I celebrated our fiftieth wedding anniversary, trekking through seven European countries. I continued to see Dr. Allen for checkups, every three months for the first year; annually, for five more years.

I'm not certain that I ever did anything to save the world, but I try to step into the fragile, and often fearful world of cancer patients, both family and friends, as they struggle through diagnosis and treatments; phone calls, visits, cards, sunflowers, or a book, chosen just for them. Sometimes I press a keepsake, a hand-blown, glass heart, into their palms, like the one a friend gave me years ago—on my way to the hospital, before surgery—to remind them:

"You will get through this. Remember, you will get through this."

15

Look Back

After our Evening Walk:

I don't remember ever calling 911 before last September when my husband complained of chest pains and shortness of breath after our evening walk. I remember that I left him sitting by the front door—in the deepening twilight—beneath the bright porch light, as moths fluttered about his head.

I remember thinking, "I don't know how to make this call with a cell phone." I remember that we had a landline phone—that we never used—on his desk, stashed behind a collection of framed family photographs. I remember picking up the unfamiliar receiver.

Alone:

I don't remember how I found the strength to walk back inside of our house after the ambulance pulled away. I remember assuring the EMT's that I would call my son and he would drive me to the nearby hospital. I remember that they were reluctant to leave me by myself. I remember how silent the house seemed after I closed the door. I remember that I had never felt so alone.

To the Rescue:

I don't remember how long I stood frozen in the darkness before three of our neighbors rang the doorbell. I remember that George and Patricia—the first neighbors we met when we moved here seven years ago—were kind and spoke gently with me. I remember that George offered to drive me to the hospital if our son couldn't. I remember that Patricia offered to spend the night, and assured me that she would pray for us.

I remember magically thinking that everything would be okay, but just in case, I remember asking for their phone numbers. I remember scrawling numerals down on the cover of a nearby book.

I remember that Eric—our known-to-be-nosy-neighbor – was also there. I remember his hesitation before he reluctantly gave up his phone number. I remember thinking, "It's just like him to be here as an ambulance chaser. I wonder how he'll spin this story tomorrow?"

One More Time:

I don't remember how many days elapsed between Steve's first hospitalization and the evening that he had a seizure in our family room.

I remember asking, "Are you okay?" after his eyes locked into a fixed stare, and his left arm and hand began to tremble and twitch, as I watched helplessly. When the seizure ended, I remember asking, "Did you feel that?" I remember him weakly nodding his head.

Disappearance:

I don't remember if I even had to identify myself or give the operator my address, the second time I called 911. I remember an efficient female voice, "The ambulance is on its way. They're three minutes away. They should be on your street right now."

I remember the same three EMT's hovering over Steve, monitoring his blood pressure, heart rate, and muscle tone. I remember them telling me, "You did the right thing, calling us."

After the ambulance sped away, I remember that one of them—who had arrived in a separate aid car—walked me back to our front door. As if to cheer me up, he smiled and asked, "Who's the gardener? Your flowers sure are beautiful."

I remember that I could hardly speak. "I do the planning, some of the planting, but he does most of it, even sets up the drip system whenever we leave," pointing to the ambulance as it disappeared around the corner with Steve inside.

Another Language:

I don't remember how many tests Steve was subjected to after I arrived in the emergency room. I remember hearing unfamiliar medical terms that would soon meld into our daily language: Uncontrolled Atrial Fibrillation. Transient Ischemic Attacks. Bacterial Pneumonia. Pericardial Effusion.

I remember voices, "You need to go home now and get some rest. We're going to take good care of him. Don't worry."

I remember a weary-looking volunteer at the intake help desk—who looked up as I wandered out of the emergency room—and called, "Have a nice evening." I remember that it was 3:00 a.m.

May You Be Safe:

I don't remember if I showered, or brushed my teeth, or combed my hair, or even changed out of the clothes I slept in before I returned to the hospital the next morning. I remember that Steve wanted me to hold him, to climb in alongside him, on his narrow hospital bed.

I remembered the last single bed we had squeezed ourselves into. I remembered us giggling in Spain—on the Costa del Sol—one winter while traveling in search of sunshine. I remembered an unexpected European cold front, so severe that we had to cling to each other in a single bed to stay warm, to survive, to get through the night.

I remember rearranging his life-saving tubes and monitors around us as I nestled down next to him. I remember my panic, my fear, and finally, a mantra to whisper in his ear,

"May you be safe,
May you be happy,
May you be healthy,
May you live with ease."

Recall:

I don't remember the names of all the cardiologists, neurologists, rheumatologists, radiologists, residents, nurses, and aides who contributed to Steve's recovery.

I remember that our daughter's flight from San Francisco arrived late—in the middle of the night—and she insisted on going straight to the hospital to see her father.

I remember our grandchildren, peeping around the corner, as their Poppa was wheeled out of the cardiac center after a risky, but successful, procedure. I remember the pictures they drew the next day; Steve, on a gurney, his torso brightly adorned with red crayoned spirals. "This is your blood, Poppa, right here in these tubes!"

I remember our son watching the Seattle Seahawks game in his father's hospital room when Steve could—at last—comfortably, sit up. I remember the next weekend when the Huskies won. I remember Steve smiling, proudly wearing his purple and gold Washington cap.

I remember the root beer float, delivered by the hospital dietician, the first deviation from Steve's low sodium diet.

I remember buying a leather recliner to welcome him home from the hospital. I remember the exuberant sales clerk, "This model is designed for tall people. We call it the Charles Barkley chair!" I remember saying, "That will work."

Look Back:

I don't remember much else about the year 2016.

I remember that our country elected an unfit, unprepared, unhinged candidate in early November. I remember our dismay.

I remember that winter arrived early and snow lingered longer than any previous winter on record.

I remember the joyful day when Steve's cardiologist announced, "As you can, start resuming all of your normal activities. Go home. Enjoy your life!" Gesturing toward me, the doctor added, "You might want to start by taking out the garbage. This woman is worn out."

Acknowledgments

I am indebted and appreciative for the help and encouragement of many persons and organizations who have supported and influenced my writing. Thank you to:

My teachers: Marion Skurdall at South Kitsap High School; Dr. Raymond Klopsch at Pacific Lutheran University; Nick O'Connell and Priscilla Long, in the Narrative Non-fiction Program, University of Washington Outreach; and Sheila Bender, founder, teacher, and advocate, at Writing It Real, Port Townsend, WA.

The Influencers: The kind librarians aboard the Kitsap Regional Library bookmobile who overlooked the rules and allowed a young girl to check out as many books as she could carry, up the hill to her home in Harper; Fellow writers, Karen Boren Gerstenberger, who always inspires me and offers words of encouragement; Karen Robbins, who cheered me on and checked up to make sure I was writing, rather than relaxing and reading (which are also important for a writer); Ron Powers, life-long friend, fellow reader and writer, whose advice, thoughts, and insight make every sentence stronger; the wonderful writers and Board members of The Mendocino Coast Writers' Conference whose work and generosity enriched my life in northern

California; to the remarkable San Miguel Writers' Conference and Literary Festival, especially the advice of Victoria Zackheim of UCLA Extension, "Tell your readers how you feel;" and Ingemar Anderson, Tim Meikle, and the team at Kitsap Publishing whose vision, creativity and support made this book happen.

My Family: My brothers and my sister, for reading, commenting, and encouraging this project. Side-by-side, we have shared many of the moments in this book; Anna, you initiated this collection when you asked, "Mom, are we going to find all of your writing in a box in the closet someday?" Thank you for jolting me and for your fierce and loving encouragement, formatting, and editing; Paul, your gentle support has always worked, "Keep writing, Mom. You can do this." I missed a few family events, but your support kept me going; Carly, your competent ability to untangle my computer snafus always puts me back on track and calms me down. You never make me feel technologically challenged, although I really am; Songe, Knute, Krista, and Stener, you will never meet many of the people in this book, but I hope you might come to appreciate my regard for them. Write about the people in your own lives some day, or why not do it right now; And always, I appreciate the love and support of Steve, who entered my story early, and will always be my main, most beloved character.

Additional Acknowledgments

Grateful acknowledgment is also made to the editors of the anthologies listed below, in which the following chapters were first published:

"Look Back," appeared in Oasis Journal 2017: Stories, Poems, Essays by Writers over Fifty

"Ball in Play," "The Promise," and "Doc Speak," appeared in Oasis Journal 2018: Stories, Poems, Essays by Writers over Fifty.

The chapter, "Disturbing the Calm," won 1st place in the Fall/Winter 2018 Writing Contest, sponsored by Writing It Real: A Community Resource Center for Writing from Personal Experience, Port Townsend, WA; "Disturbing the Calm" shows through story and images, the thought process of changing our lives, the importance of family, and different seasons in our lives—where we begin in one place and end in another. A delightful read."   - Contest Judge

Biography

Judith Barker Kvinsland, a retired teacher and college administrator in both Washington and California, happily exchanged professional prose for personal essays and occasional prose poems. She now lives and writes in eastern Washington amidst wide-open skies, ancient, channeled scablands and burgeoning wineries. She and her husband are "itinerant  grandparents," frequent travelers to the forested beauty of northern California, Montana, and the Olympic Peninsula to connect with grandchildren and extended family.